Beach Glass

Kelly Alana Swift

Copyright © 2010, 2011, 2012, 2014, 2019

Kelly Alana Swift

All Rights Reserved.

Without limiting the under copyright, no part of this document may be reproduced, stored in or introduced into a document retrieval system, or transmitted in any form or by any means (electronic, mechanical, photocopying, recording, or otherwise), or for any purpose, without the express written permission of Kelly Alana Swift.

Second Edition print © 2020.

First edition printed © 2012.

Poem Credit: "Cali"

first appeared in Twentysomething Teenager *(discontinued)*

© 2014 Kelly Alana Swift

Poem Credit: "About The Moon," "Like Colors"

also appeared in Merging Visions: Collections III

© 2013 Denton Poets' Assembly and Visual Arts Society of Texas

Poem Credit: "Urban Skyward"

also appeared in Merging Visions: Collections IV

© 2014 Denton Poets' Assembly and Visual Arts Society of Texas

For Mom, Tom, and a few from the past.

Table of Contents

Haiku Valentines: Sunrise	8
Beach Glass	9
Haiku Valentines: Bootprints	10
Baby Brother	11
Haiku Valentines: How You Smile	13
About The Moon	14
Haiku Valentines: So Faithful	15
For My Mother's Mother, Whose Strength Only Natural Forces Could Match	16
Haiku Valentines: Spring Dreams	18
Urban Skyward	19
Haiku Valentines: Snowmen	20
I Want a Boat	21

Table of Contents, *cont.*

Haiku Valentines: Small Angel	23
Jubilation	24
Haiku Valentines: My Subtle Contours	25
Like Colors	26
Haiku Valentines: Little Tracks	27
Cali	28
Haiku Valentines: Icicles Soften	29
Easter Baby	30
Haiku Valentines: Cool Moon	31

Haiku Valentines: Sunrise

Sunrise golds our legs
entwined - ah, waking with you
before you were mine

Beach Glass

We pocketed our innocence and carried it like stones
washed ashore up those sawdust-slick stairs, dusk
retiring heavily all around us in a house some privileged child
will run room to room to room to billiard room to theater room
and perhaps never know the creative poverty
of adult siblings searching
for a hidden sunset on which to get stoned.

Beach glass, I would later learn, is old bottle shards
returned to our bare sandy feet decades later,
smoothed and reshaped by the seas, holding
each glowing summer for eternity. Precious litter.

Our feet, abandoned, dangled from the balcony as we exhaled
philosophy to the sun yawning across the highway, and I am
trying to remember seashells, pebbles carved from
dead things, my youth combing soggy shorelines,
feeling only the foam in my toes,
keeping only the prettiest bygones.

Haiku Valentines: Bootprints

Bootprints side-by-side
steering home, children stomping
deep hearts in the snow

Baby Brother
for Thomas

In a bleary September haze,
Mom let you break from her,
the last fruit from a drying tree,
flushed and slick with her interior, afraid
to thunk on the ground without everything
you thought you needed. You surfaced
in the fog, hairless blinking animal,
and reached grabby raccoon hands
for the wilderness surrounding you,
all the thorny things
babies shouldn't touch.

You are almost twenty now, a man
broadening your shoulders and striding you resolutely
out of the state, taller and stronger and faster
than all of us. Your bedroom
is tidy and fresh, absent of you
and your pungent boyish pits and your
unexpected cracking smile. You are fading
back into the mist, as am I, and we're
leaving her in the looming cavernous house,
prey to the insatiable frustration
boxing its walls like a bear
who's forgotten how to fish. You don't need
her anymore, and soon, nor will I -

but on that first day, she could cradle you
in her freckled mother arms, whole, and knew
all the answers you needed, familiar cub
with hungry lips and Dad's persuasive
blue eyes, slimy plump red other beacon
to Mom's elusive joy.

Haiku Valentines: How You Smile

How you smile and how
my pulse flutters and oh, how
we fit curved like spoons

About The Moon

"Write me a poem," you request,
low tide eyes

to the shimmering heavens, "about precise shadows
fluttering on lacteous grass, our spirited chorus
reawakening the porch, hanging bulbs glittering
joyous holidays in August.

"Write about stillness
so quiet

one can hear leaves whispering
friction like fingers revering silken hair,
traffic respiring in the distance, the wet language
only our lips have learned, explosive
atoms smashing between us.

"Write me a poem," you smile,
"about the moon."

Haiku Valentines: So Faithful

So faithful, secure,
the last button fastened
before braving the blizzard

For My Mother's Mother, Whose Strength Only Natural Forces Could Match

You are done, you declare,
reclining like a helpless thing, hemmed by fine
metal pins to this cramped fluorescent room,
spitting piss and vinegar at plastic tubes
tentacling into your thin weathered husk. You're done,
you vow, done with all of this, deaf at nurses
instructing you how to avert the hooded
inevitable sitting with us as we chatter all day,
laughing about our lives as sane people.

Your broad smile is ours.
Your mortality is hers
and mine.

Tornado alley isn't soft on aging goats
whose decades amiable coastal breezes
caressed; your stubbornness buckled
under your bad knee and here you sulk,
swinging counterpunches, done with wind,
done with caned putters to the morning paper,
done with this restless southern sky
denying you respite. On the complacent rise
of the dawn of your last breath, the same
glimmering copper sun will wheel up
a Garden Grove sidewalk, uncompromising as you,

to Oklahoma across the ferocious, gusting planet -

but you're not finished yet.

Haiku Valentines: Spring Dreams

Spring dreams beneath silk
quilts asparkle, until from
the frost, a flower

Urban Skyward

Northbound and inward and sideways and plastic
tumbleweeding across a parking lot, a good friend's voice
unspooling balmily from consonants, bookends spreading
and being taken down, beauty
drifts skyward
to this brazen bloodshot sunset
radiating through bombastic silhouettes stacked high
above what grew here first. Beauty, you remind me, easing
the crescendo of blond straw orbiting my shoes,
calmly
respires
in everything. Even
the polylegged arachnids
weaving intangible conundrums in every corner of my home.

Haiku Valentines: Snowmen

Instead, snowmen strolled
the town, shook twig hands, nuzzled
blithe carrot noses

I Want a Boat

or small yacht. I want to unlatch my rope
to land, to the mundane chaos
and routines, the throng of tidy hair and suits
rushing through steel and glass obligations, cell phones
prattling in every ear, myopic machine parts all
missing the midday reflecting off concrete, birds
feeding their young in the fluorescent loops of
store signs, flowers drooping dismally, lost animals
in need of a meal and a good scratch, or their
home back. I want to be buoyed
offbalance like a jovial drunk and sleep
underwater, my subconscious dark
or Malibu blue or cerulean-grey during a thunderstorm,
bustling with tens of billions of sparkling eyes
curious about me, about how I eat
with a fork and brush my unsharp
omnivore teeth and lay on my bed
watching their undulating scales and fins glow
across my window, a multicultural ecosystem
I'll never know if I stay inside
this painted wood nailed together, detached
from mild afternoons and wrathful rainfall, safe
and dry. I want a sunburn like catching fire
so I can peel back my old skins
and roll them like eraser crumbs
in my fingers, rejoicing in the wrinkles

my grin squinches under my eyes,
because I am no longer boring
or bored. I never want unwindblown
hair again, dry toes or shoulders,
asphalt destinations or mechanically rattling
journeys without the friendly hello of seagulls
swooping from Heaven, another evening sun
not a crimson and gold God, that which makes life
possible, but a heatlamp
cooking us like veal and drying out our existence.
I want to swim without ingesting
chlorine, to find my grandfather's joyous
sea eyes within my own, and I want to breathe,
I want to breathe
clean Earth air.

Haiku Valentines: Small Angel

Small angel twitching,
puppy glows warm by the fire,
exhales doughy Z's

Jubilation

When I swelled to the sextillion
winking eyes of the stars and said,
"I love you," I meant it.
Each syllable, each sound,
wee lightning bugs flitting about the intimate night,
is a gift I capture in these lips, on this
thirsty tongue and close in mason jars
with tiny holes toothpicked in their lids
for you. I am a jubilant child always
in the starshine of your grin, a woman
beneath your lucky hands, and when I swell
again and again and say, "I love you,"
I still mean
every word.

Haiku Valentines: My Subtle Contours

My subtle contours
in the dark, live nerve endings
your opaque face learns

Like Colors

Since before corrosive lye scrunched the first
soiled garments, our souls were meant
to converge here
in this rattling concrete laundromat
perspiring lethargy at the height of summer
or hardening our bones in bottomless winter.

You, oldest and dearest friend, embrace
like warm fabrics tumbling from the dryer,
cozy on my cheek. You are abrupt clouds
of fragrant detergent, the spin cycle
rolling and rolling as we watch.

What we talk about doesn't matter.
Your rough hands fold efficiently, airy eyes
brighten when I laugh. Before the first
load of laundry and before time, I was meant
to fasten to you, slow as the earth whirled, admire
your static cling to my senses,
like colors seeping to fresh sheets.

Haiku Valentines: Little Tracks

Little tracks dotting
milky rooftops: lost mousers
crunching to shelter

Cali

My finicky cat would adjust
to relocation; that's not

the problem. The problem is everyone
else in the know who crawl rampant every

square inch of budding chaparral, undulating desert,
warm sand which fills the body's abandoned spaces,

vital blood sun
returning home across the cawing ocean,

salty breezes exhaling soul from temporary flesh
on the PCH. We need this. Real estate costs your

working organs and commuting is a clogged artery; still,
it's this simple: When you leave, you leave

yourself. Cool nights, when most traffic sleeps,
the earth quakes us alive with subtle stirs

reorienting our smog-waywarded consciousness. Cali
softens our cores and grows us each a buttery poppy.

Haiku Valentines: Icicles Soften

Icicles soften,
weep to the wide wanting porch,
until your return

Easter Baby

Everyday is my birthday, every touch
and smile and peck on the cheek
my favorite gift. I love
to love you, face the budding sun,
weightless being welcoming springtime,
discovering florid eggs like giddy secrets
just for me, and I float with the easy levity
of childhood - I am the luckiest little girl
skipping in clicking heels and a pretty pink
Easter dress - I am the luckiest little girl
in the whole wide wonderful world.

Haiku Valentines: Cool Moon

Cool moon tucks itself
in velour clouds, drops its eyes:
goodnight, snow, goodnight

Born April 19, 1987, Kelly Alana Swift has been passionately creating since she could hold a crayon. Her self-published works include *Beach Glass* (2012) and *Life Manual* (2016), re-released as new editions in 2020; *Twentysomething Teenager* (2014, discontinued); *Built 1987: New and Selected Poems* (2020); and *Bonfire* (2020). She currently lives in Fort Worth, Texas, with supportive family and her beloved cat, Kara.

Made in the USA
Coppell, TX
22 August 2021